COME, THOU
FOUNT
OF EVERY
*blessing*

# COME, THOU FOUNT OF EVERY blessing

MESSAGES of REDEMPTION IN SCRIPTURE AND VERSE

PLAIN SIGHT PUBLISHING
AN IMPRINT OF CEDAR FORT, INC.
SPRINGVILLE, UTAH

ANGELA D. BAXTER

ISBN 13: 978-1-4621-1594-5

Published by Plain Sight Publishing, an imprint of Cedar Fort, Inc.
2373 W. 700 S., Springville, UT 84663
Distributed by Cedar Fort, Inc., www.cedarfort.com

Library of Congress Control Number: 2015937684

Cover and page design by Angela D. Baxter
Edited by Eileen Leavitt
Cover design © 2015 by Lyle Mortimer

Printed in China

10  9  8  7  6  5  4  3  2  1

Printed on acid-free paper

*for* ALISHA

# blessing

*n.* \bless·ing\

1. *Approval that allows or helps you to do something*

2. *Help and approval from God*

3. *Something that helps you or brings happiness*

**R**OBERT ROBINSON was twenty-two when he wrote the lyrics to the hymn "Come, Thou Fount of Every Blessing." It was 1757, and Robinson was a brilliant young Methodist minister in Norwich, England. The hymn is in many ways Robinson's personal prayer and his testimony of his life, conversion, and desire for forgiveness and redemption. "Come, Thou Fount" is a hymn of praise to God for all the blessings He has bestowed and a prayer asking Him to bring people everywhere to repentance and to form us more into His likeness, sealing our hearts unto Him in preparation of the eternal glory to come.

Robert Robinson was born in Norfolk, England, in 1735. His father died when Robinson was young, leaving the family in poverty. After a few years, Robinson's mother found herself unable to control the increasingly difficult Robert. He was sent to London at age fourteen in the hopes that he would grow into a responsible adult through an apprenticeship to a barber. However, Robert spent more time reading, drinking, and making trouble with the local gangs than working.

When he was seventeen, Robinson and some friends attended a revival meeting, intending to mock those in attendance. Instead, when the great evangelist George Whitefield began to preach, his impassioned sermon had a great influence on the wayward Robinson, who recognized his need for repentance. Haunted by Whitefield's words for the next three years, Robinson eventually became a Methodist preacher himself. Two years into his ministry, he would write the hymn expressing his joy in his newfound faith, "Come, Thou Fount of Every Blessing."

In 1759, Robinson left the Methodist church and became a Baptist, spending nearly thirty years as pastor of Stone-Yard Baptist Church in Cambridge, England. Robinson's hymn seems to have been prophetic of his later years, because once again he seemed to drift away from his faith and his God. His life became characterized by lapses into sin and unstableness. He was also accused of believing the doctrines of Unitarianism, which, among other things, doubts the full divinity of Christ.

The story is told that Robinson once encountered a woman on a stagecoach who spoke of a particular hymn and the blessing it had brought to her soul. She asked Robinson what he thought of the hymn she had been humming. He tearfully said, "Madam, I am the poor unhappy man who wrote that hymn many years ago, and I would give a thousand worlds, if I had them, to enjoy the feelings I had then."

It is said that she comforted Robinson, replying, "Sir, the 'streams of mercy' are still flowing." Robinson was deeply moved.

"Come, Thou Fount of Every Blessing" is commonly set to the tune "Nettleton," written by printer and lay musician John Wyeth. The hymn was published in Wyeth's collection of folk hymns in 1813 and is among the most popular hymns today. It continues to stand as an inspiring prayer for personal redemption.

## SOURCES

Burrage, Henry. *Baptist Hymn Writers and their Hymns*. Portland, MN: Brown Thurston and Co., 1888.

*Merriam-Webster Online*, s.v. "blessing," accessed June 3, 2015, www.merriam-webster.com/dictionary/blessing.

Morgan, Robert J. *Then Sings My Soul: 150 of the World's Greatest Hymn Stories*. Nashville, TN: Thomas Nelson, Inc., 2003.

Osbeck, Kenneth. *101 Hymn Stories*. Grand Rapids, MI: Kregel Publications, 1982.

COME,
THOU
*fount*

**J**ESUS ANSWERED and said unto her, Whosoever drinketh of this water shall thirst again:

BUT WHOSOEVER drinketh of the water that I shall give him shall never thirst; but the water that I shall give him shall be in him a well of water springing up into everlasting life.

JOHN 4:13–14

# PROVE ME NOW

herewith, saith the Lord of hosts, if I will not open you the windows of heaven, and pour you out a blessing, that there shall not be room enough to receive it.

MALACHI 3:10

TUNE MY

*heart*

# FOR THE LORD seeth

not as man seeth; for man looketh on

the outward appearance, but the Lord

looketh on the heart.

## 1 SAMUEL 16:7

# SING, O HEAVENS;

and be joyful, O earth; and break forth into singing, O mountains: for the Lord hath comforted his people, and will have mercy upon his afflicted.

ISAIAH 49:13

# TO SING Thy GRACE

STREAMS
OF
mercy

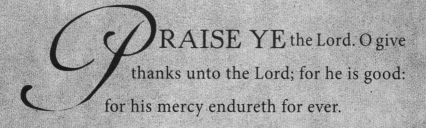

PRAISE YE the Lord. O give thanks unto the Lord; for he is good: for his mercy endureth for ever.

PSALM 106:1

# I

T IS OF the Lord's mercies that we
are not consumed, because his compassions
fail not.
THEY ARE NEW every morning:
great is thy faithfulness.

LAMENTATIONS 3:22–23

*never*
CEASING

CALL FOR *songs* OF LOUDEST PRAISE

**B**UT I WILL SING of thy power; yea, I will sing aloud of thy mercy in the morning: for thou hast been my defence and refuge in the day of my trouble.

PSALM 59:16

# Make a joyful

noise unto the Lord, all ye lands.

**SERVE THE LORD** with gladness: come before his presence with singing. . . .

**FOR THE LORD** is good; his mercy is everlasting; and his truth endureth to all generations.

PSALM 100:1–2, 5

TEACH ME SOME *melodious* SONNET

SUNG BY

FLAMING

TONGUES

*above*

**T**HE LORD THY God in the midst of thee is mighty; he will save, he will rejoice over thee with joy; he will rest in his love, he will joy over thee with singing.

ZEPHANIAH 3:17

SING, O YE heavens; for the Lord hath done it: shout, ye lower parts of the earth: break forth into singing, ye mountains, O forest, and every tree therein: for the Lord hath redeemed Jacob, and glorified himself in Israel.

ISAIAH 44:23

# PRAISE THE *mount*

I'M

# FIXED

*upon*

IT

*T*HEREFORE, my beloved brethren, be ye steadfast, unmoveable, always abounding in the work of the Lord, forasmuch as ye know that your labour is not in vain in the Lord.

## 1 CORINTHIANS 15:58

MOUNT OF THY REDEEMING love

HEAR MY CRY, O God; attend unto my prayer.

FROM THE END of the earth will I cry unto thee, when my heart is overwhelmed: lead me to the rock that is higher than I.

PSALM 61:1–2

Blessed be god, even the Father of our Lord Jesus Christ, the Father of mercies, and the God of all comfort;

who comforteth us in all our tribulation, that we may be able to comfort them which are in any trouble, by the comfort wherewith we ourselves are comforted of God.

2 CORINTHIANS 1:3–4

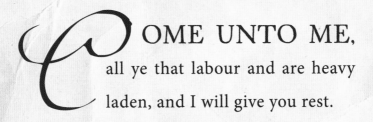

OME UNTO ME, all ye that labour and are heavy laden, and I will give you rest.

MATTHEW 11:28

TILL *released*

FROM *flesh* AND *sin*

So WHEN this corruptible shall have put on incorruption, and this mortal shall have put on immortality, then shall be brought to pass the saying that is written, Death is swallowed up in victory.

O DEATH, where is thy sting? O grave, where is thy victory?

1 CORINTHIANS 15:54–55

*T*HEN SHALL the King say unto them on his right hand, Come, ye blessed of my Father, inherit the kingdom prepared for you from the foundation of the world.

MATTHEW 25:34

YET *from*

WHAT I DO

*inherit*

HERE THY *praises* I'LL BEGIN

**I** WILL GREATLY rejoice in the Lord, my soul shall be joyful in my God; for he hath clothed me with the garments of salvation, he hath covered me with the robe of righteousness.

ISAIAH 61:10

**A**ND SAMUEL SPAKE unto all the house of Israel, saying, If ye do return unto the Lord with all your hearts, . . . and serve him only: and he will deliver you. . . .

THEN SAMUEL took a stone, and set it between Mizpeh and Shen, and called the name of it Eben-ezer, saying, Hitherto hath the Lord helped us.

1 SAMUEL 7:3, 12

HERE I raise MY Ebenezer

HERE BY THY GREAT

*help*

I'VE COME

# GOD IS OUR refuge and strength, a very present help in trouble. THEREFORE WILL NOT we fear, though the earth be removed, and though the mountains be carried into the midst of the sea; THOUGH THE WATERS thereof roar and be troubled, though the mountains shake with the swelling thereof. Selah.

PSALM 46:1–3

*B*LESSED is the man that trusteth in the Lord, and whose hope the Lord is.

JEREMIAH 17:7

BY *Thy* GOOD *pleasure*

*A*ND WE know that all things work together for good to them that love God, to them who are the called according to his purpose.

ROMANS 8:28

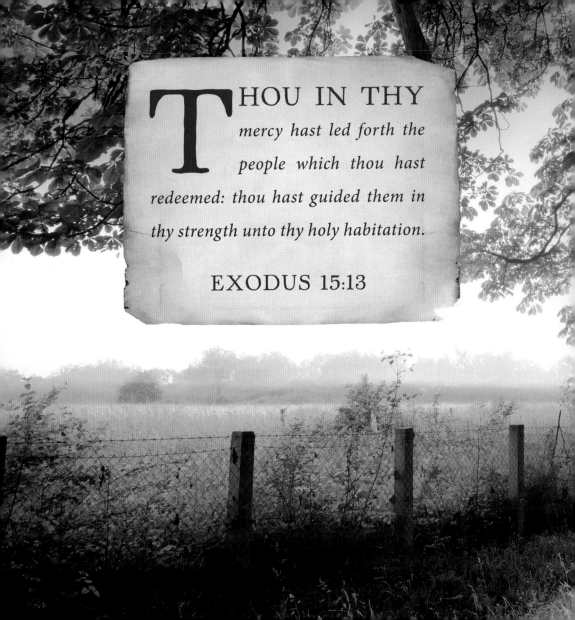

THOU IN THY mercy hast led forth the people which thou hast redeemed: thou hast guided them in thy strength unto thy holy habitation.

EXODUS 15:13

# SAFELY
## TO ARRIVE
### AT
*home*

**F**EAR THOU NOT; for I am
with thee: be not dismayed; for I am
thy God: I will strengthen thee; yea, I
will help thee; yea, I will uphold thee with the
right hand of my righteousness.

ISAIAH 41:10

*F*OR I WAS an hungred, and ye gave me meat: I was thirsty, and ye gave me drink: I was a stranger, and ye took me in: NAKED, AND YE CLOTHED ME: I was sick, and ye visited me: I was in prison, and ye came unto me.

MATTHEW 25:35–36

# WHEN

## A

# stranger

# WANDERING FROM THE *fold* OF GOD

**I**F A MAN HAVE an hundred sheep, and one of them be gone astray, doth he not leave the ninety and nine, and goeth into the mountains, and seeketh that which is gone astray?

AND IF SO BE that he find it, verily I say unto you, he rejoiceth more of that sheep, than of the ninety and nine which went not astray.

MATTHEW 18:12–13

*T*HERE HATH no temptation taken you but such as is common to man: but God is faithful, who will not suffer you to be tempted above that ye are able; but will with the temptation also make a way to escape, that ye may be able to bear it.

1 CORINTHIANS 10:13

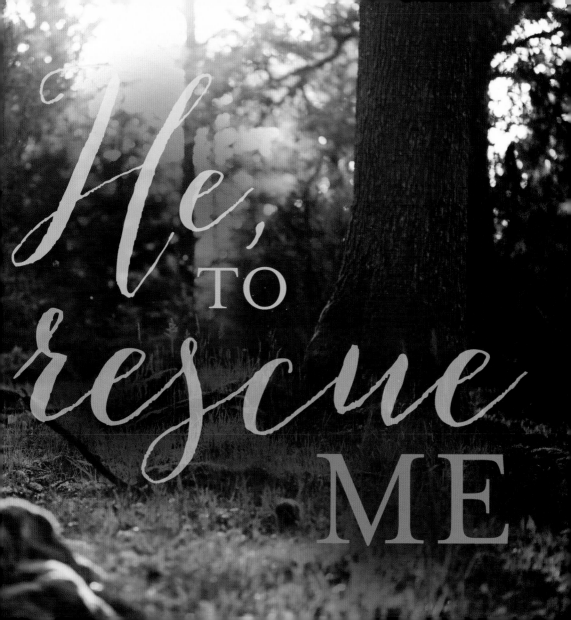

*He, to rescue me*

FROM *danger,*

**W**HO IS A God like unto thee, that pardoneth iniquity, and passeth by the transgression of the remnant of his heritage? he retaineth not his anger for ever, because he delighteth in mercy.

**HE WILL TURN** again, he will have compassion upon us; he will subdue our iniquities; and thou wilt cast all their sins into the depths of the sea.

MICAH 7:18–19

# SURELY HE HATH borne

our griefs, and carried our sorrows: yet we did esteem him stricken, smitten of God, and afflicted.

# BUT HE WAS WOUNDED

for our transgressions, he was bruised for our iniquities: the chastisement of our peace was upon him; and with his stripes we are healed.

ISAIAH 53:4–5

# INTERPOSED HIS *precious* BLOOD

HOW **HIS**

*kindness*

BUT LET HIM that glorieth glory in this, that he understandeth and knoweth me, that I am the Lord which exercise lovingkindness, judgment, and righteousness, in the earth: for in these things I delight, saith the Lord.

JEREMIAH 9:24

Therefore if any man be in Christ, he is a new creature: old things are passed away; behold, all things are become new.

2 CORINTHIANS 5:17

YET *pursues* ME

*mortal* TONGUE CAN *never* TELL

**B**UT AS IT IS WRITTEN, Eye hath not seen, nor ear heard, neither have entered into the heart of man, the things which God hath prepared for them that love him.

1 CORINTHIANS 2:9

BUT WE HAVE this treasure in earthen vessels, that the excellency of the power may be of God, and not of us.

WE ARE TROUBLED on every side, yet not distressed; we are perplexed, but not in despair;

PERSECUTED, BUT NOT forsaken; cast down, but not destroyed.

2 CORINTHIANS 4:7–9

# clothed
## IN FLESH

TILL

*death*

SHALL

*loose*

ME

Nor height, nor depth,
nor any other creature, shall be able
to separate us from the love of God,
which is in Christ Jesus our Lord.

ROMANS 8:39

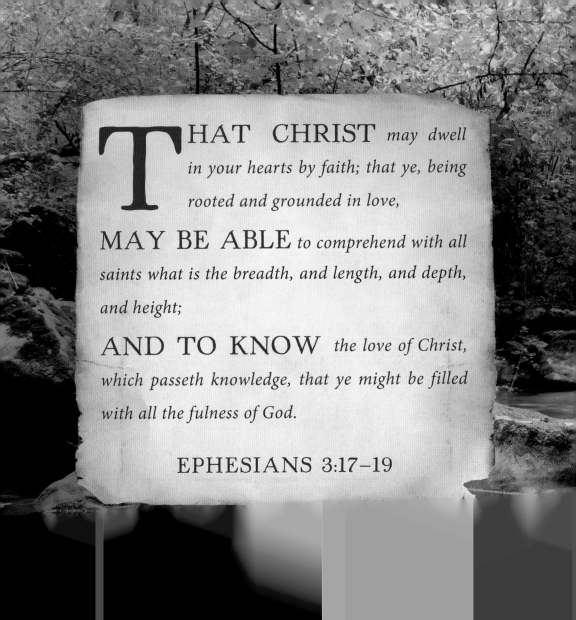

**T**HAT CHRIST *may dwell in your hearts by faith; that ye, being rooted and grounded in love,*

MAY BE ABLE *to comprehend with all saints what is the breadth, and length, and depth, and height;*

AND TO KNOW *the love of Christ, which passeth knowledge, that ye might be filled with all the fulness of God.*

EPHESIANS 3:17–19

I cannot PROCLAIM IT well

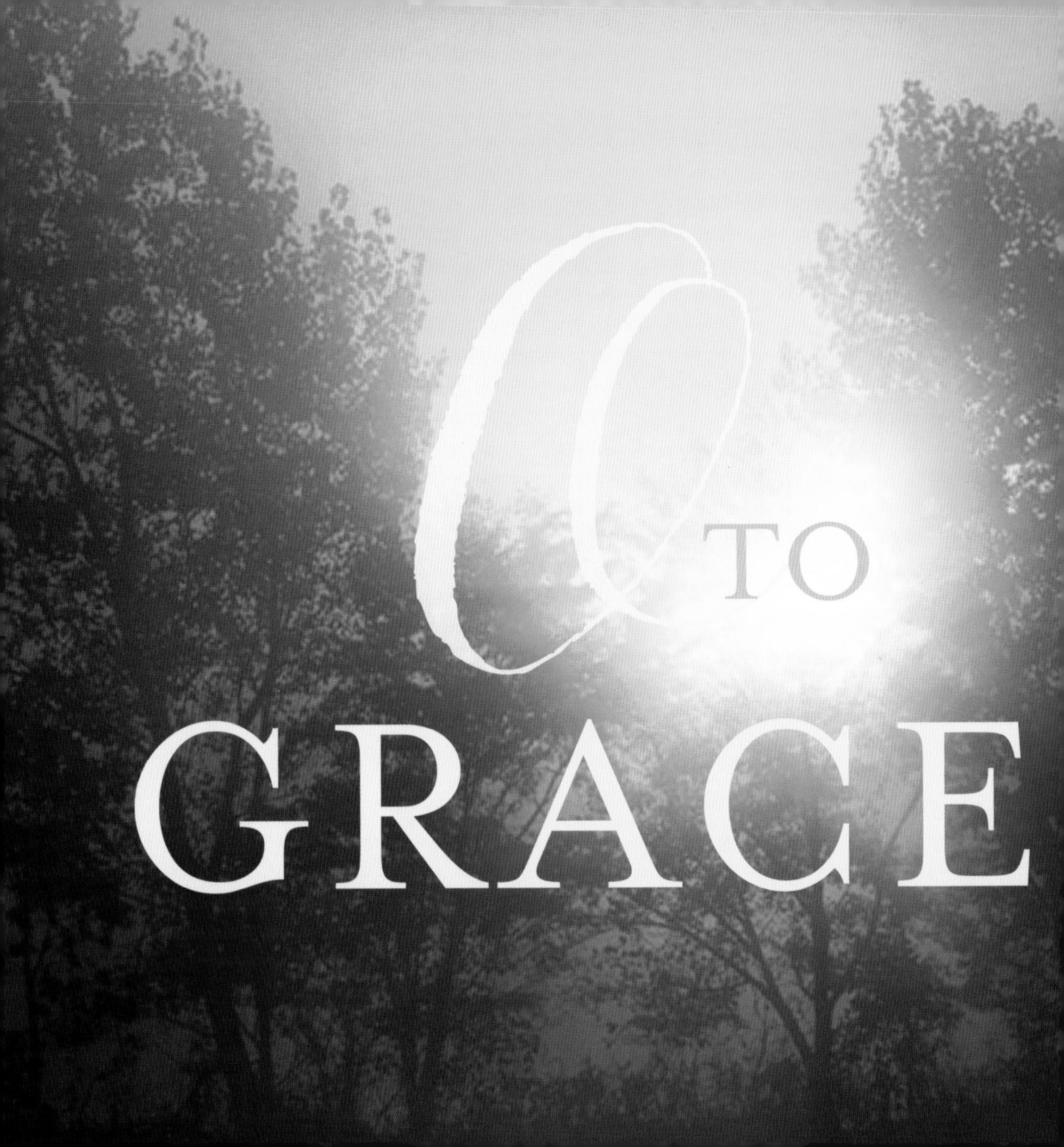
O
TO
GRACE

**F**OR BY GRACE are ye saved through faith; and that not of yourselves: it is the gift of God.

EPHESIANS 2:8

AND HE SAID unto me, My grace is sufficient for thee: for my strength is made perfect in weakness. Most gladly therefore will I rather glory in my infirmities, that the power of Christ may rest upon me.

2 CORINTHIANS 12:9

# HOW
# GREAT
# A
# *debtor*

DAILY I'M *constrained* TO BE

# KEEP YOURSELVES

in the love of God, looking for the mercy of our Lord Jesus Christ unto eternal life.

## JUDE 1:21

**H**E RESTORETH

my soul: he leadeth me in the paths of

righteousness for his name's sake.

PSALM 23:3

# LIKE
## A
## *feller,*

# FOR THE MOUNTAINS

shall depart, and the hills be removed; but my kindness shall not depart from thee, neither shall the covenant of my peace be removed, saith the Lord that hath mercy on thee.

## ISAIAH 54:10

**T**RUST IN THE Lord with all thine heart; and lean not unto thine own understanding.

**IN ALL THY** ways acknowledge him, and he shall direct thy paths.

PROVERBS 3:5–6

BIND MY wandering HEART

TO

Thee

*J*ESUS SAID unto her, I am the resurrection, and the life: he that believeth in me, though he were dead, yet shall he live.

AND WHOSOEVER liveth and believeth in me shall never die.

JOHN 11:25–26

# ALL WE LIKE SHEEP

have gone astray; we have turned every one to his own way; and the Lord hath laid on him the iniquity of us all.

## ISAIAH 53:6

PRONE

TO

*wander,*

# I

**EVEN I,** am he that blotteth out thy transgressions for mine own sake, and will not remember thy sins.

**PUT ME IN** remembrance: let us plead together: declare thou, that thou mayest be justified.

ISAIAH 43:25–26

AND, HAVING made peace through the blood of his cross, by him to reconcile all things unto himself . . .

AND YOU, that were sometime alienated and enemies in your mind by wicked works, yet now hath he reconciled in the body of his flesh through death, to present you holy and unblameable and unreproveable in his sight.

COLOSSIANS 1:20–22

# PRONE
## TO
# leave

# THE
# GOD
## I
# *love*

*A*ND NOW, Israel, what doth the Lord thy God require of thee, but to fear the Lord thy God, to walk in all his ways, and to love him, and to serve the Lord thy God with all thy heart and with all thy soul.

DEUTERONOMY 10:12

# W

ITH MY WHOLE heart have I sought thee: O let me not wander from thy commandments.

PSALM 119:10

HERE'S MY *heart*

A NEW HEART also will I give you, and a new spirit will I put within you: and I will take away the stony heart out of your flesh, and I will give you an heart of flesh.

EZEKIEL 36:26

# SEAL IT *for*

NOW HE *which stablisheth us with you in Christ, and hath anointed us, is God;* WHO HATH ALSO *sealed us, and given the earnest of the Spirit in our hearts.*

## 2 CORINTHIANS 1:21–22

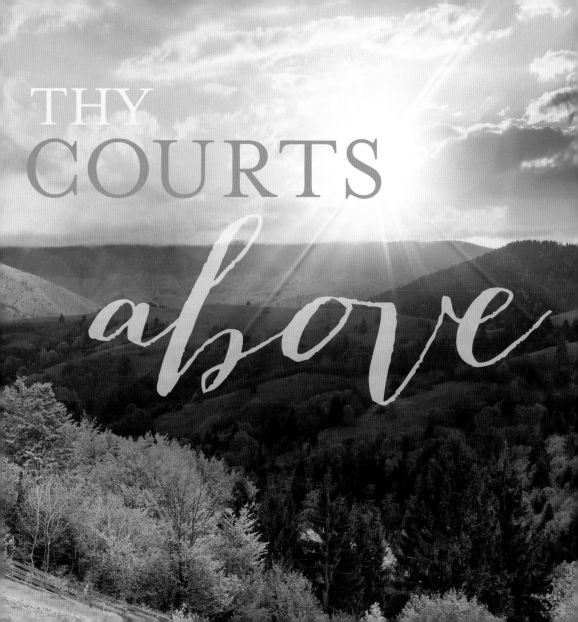

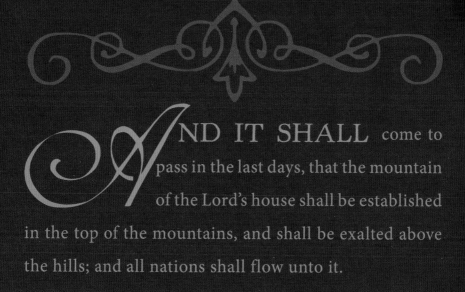

*A*ND IT SHALL come to pass in the last days, that the mountain of the Lord's house shall be established in the top of the mountains, and shall be exalted above the hills; and all nations shall flow unto it.

ISAIAH 2:2

**B**UT NOW being made free from sin, and become servants to God, ye have your fruit unto holiness, and the end everlasting life.

ROMANS 6:22

# WHEN *freed* FROM SINNING

I shall *see*

While we look not at the things which are seen, but at the things which are not seen: for the things which are seen are temporal; but the things which are not seen are eternal.

2 CORINTHIANS 4:18

# GOD BE MERCIFUL

unto us, and bless us; and cause

his face to shine upon us; Selah.

## PSALM 67:1

*clothed*
THEN

AWAKE, AWAKE; put on thy strength, O Zion; put on thy beautiful garments, O Jerusalem, the holy city: for henceforth there shall no more come into thee the uncircumcised and the unclean.

ISAIAH 52:1

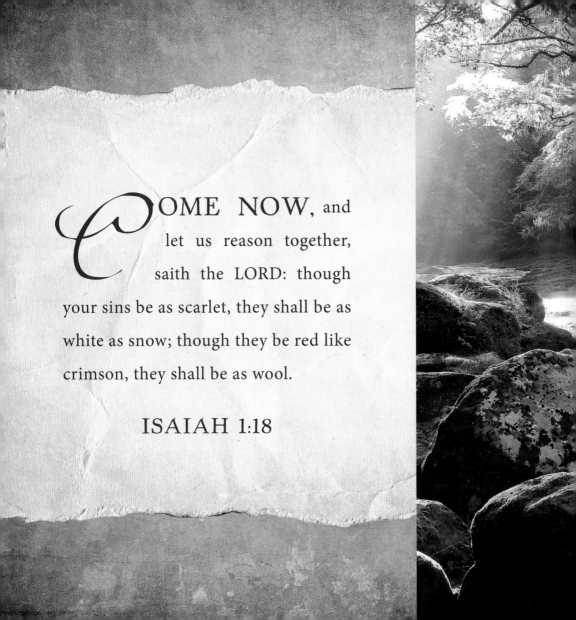

COME NOW, and let us reason together, saith the LORD: though your sins be as scarlet, they shall be as white as snow; though they be red like crimson, they shall be as wool.

ISAIAH 1:18

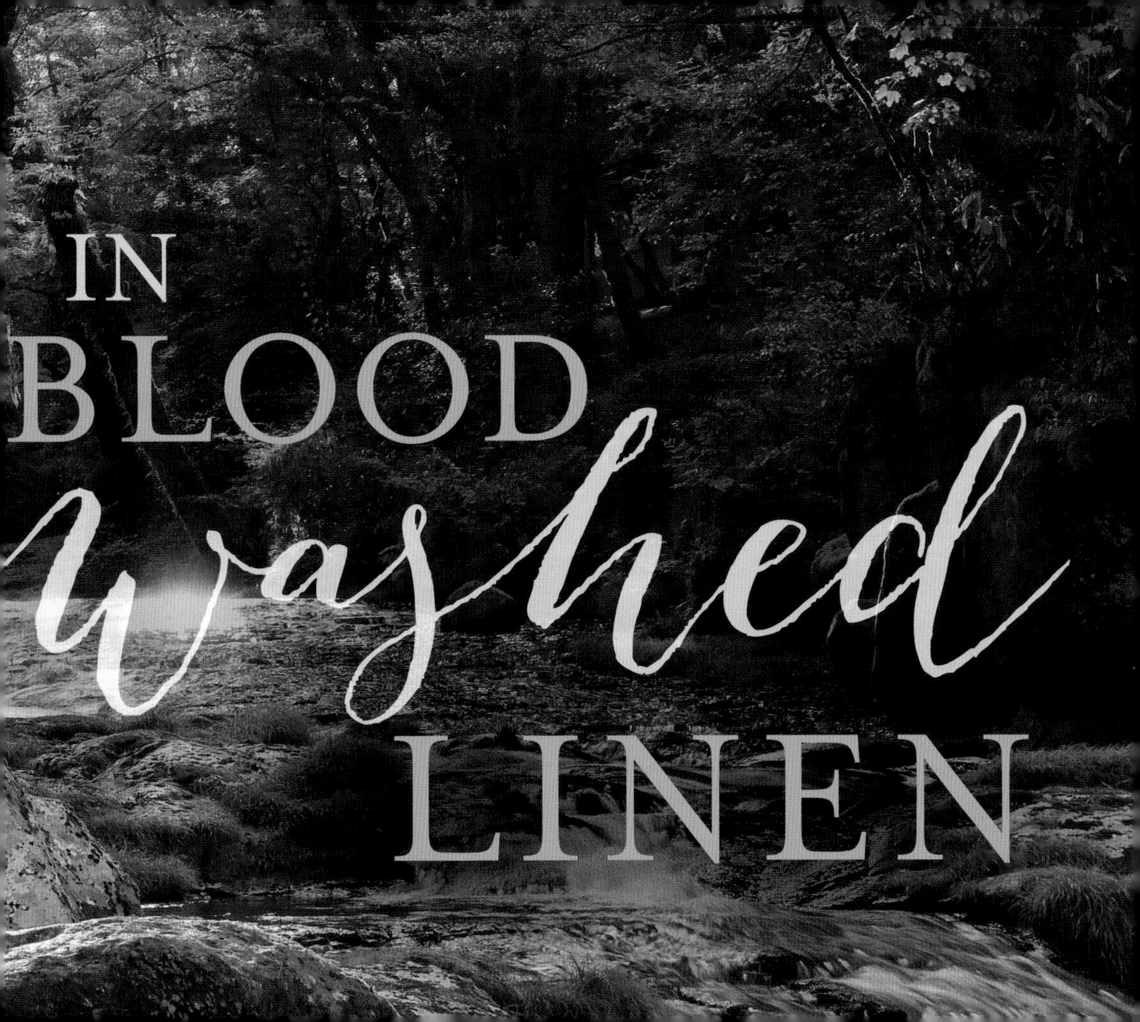

IN
BLOOD
*washed*
LINEN

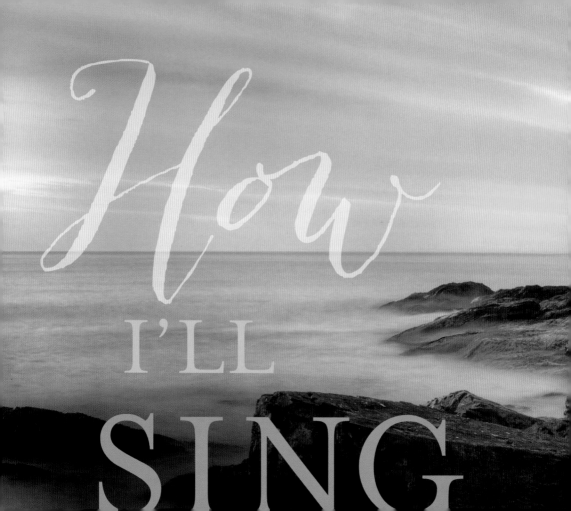

*T*HE LORD IS

my strength and song, and

he is become my salvation.

EXODUS 15:2

HAVE MERCY upon me, O God, according to thy lovingkindness: according unto the multitude of thy tender mercies blot out my transgressions.

PSALM 51:1

# THY sovereign GRACE

FOR UNTO US a child is born, unto us a son is given: and the government shall be upon his shoulder: and his name shall be called Wonderful, Counsellor, The mighty God, The everlasting Father, The Prince of Peace.

ISAIAH 9:6

*T*RULY MY SOUL waiteth upon God: from him cometh my salvation. *T*HE ONLY IS my rock and my salvation; he is my defence; I shall not be greatly moved.

PSALM 62:1–2

TAKE MY *ransomed* SOUL AWAY

O LORD, THOU hast pleaded the causes of my soul; thou hast redeemed my life.

LAMENTATIONS 3:58

*B*EHOLD, I SEND an Angel before thee, to keep thee in the way, and to bring thee into the place which I have prepared.

EXODUS 23:20

SEND

THINE

*angels*

NOW

TO *carry* ME

# ONE THING HAVE

I desired of the Lord, that will I seek after; that I may dwell in the house of the Lord all the days of my life.

PSALM 27:4

*T*HEREFORE ARE they before the throne of God, and serve him day and night in his temple: and he that sitteth on the throne shall dwell among them.

THEY SHALL HUNGER no more, neither thirst any more; neither shall the sun light on them, nor any heat.

FOR THE LAMB which is in the midst of the throne shall feed them, and shall lead them unto living fountains of waters: and God shall wipe away all tears from their eyes.

REVELATION 7:15–17

TO realms

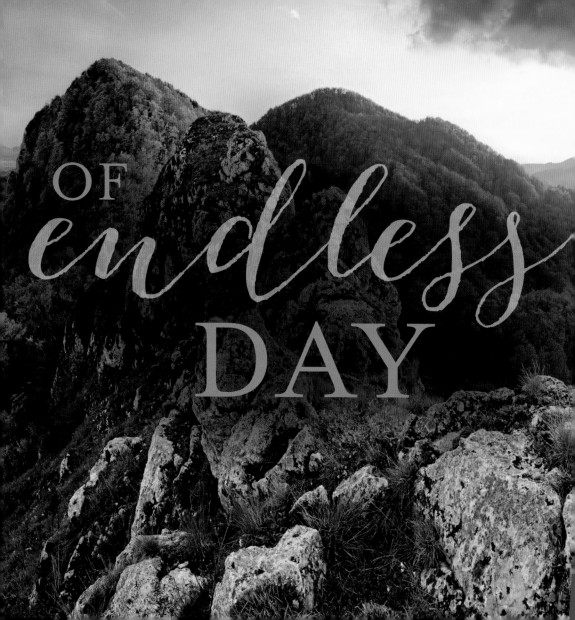

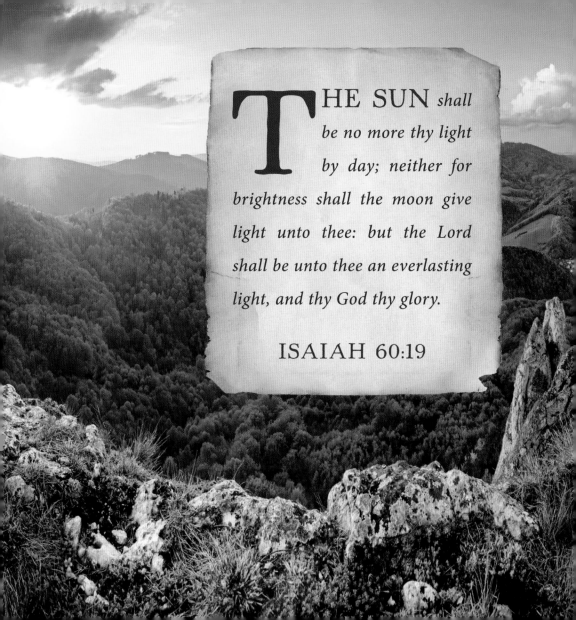

# Come, Thou Fount of Every Blessing

Robert Robinson.

John Wyeth.

1. Come, Thou Fount of ev-'ry bless-ing, Tune my heart to sing Thy grace;
2. Sorrow-ing I shall be in spir-it, Till re-leased from flesh and sin,

Streams of mer-cy, nev-er ceas-ing, Call for songs of loud-est praise.
Yet from what I do in-her-it, Here Thy prais-es I'll be-gin;

Teach me some me-lo-dious son-net, Sung by flam-ing tongues a-bove.
Here I raise my Eb-en-e-zer; Here by Thy great help I've come;

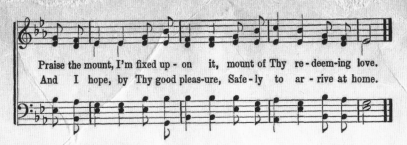

Praise the mount, I'm fixed up - on it, mount of Thy re - deem - ing love.
And I hope, by Thy good pleas - ure, Safe - ly to ar - rive at home.

3. Jesus sought me when a stranger,
   Wandering from the fold of God;
   He, to rescue me from danger,
   Interposed His precious blood;
   How His kindness yet pursues me
   Mortal tongue can never tell,
   Clothed in flesh, till death shall loose me
   I cannot proclaim it well.

4. O to grace how great a debtor
   Daily I'm constrained to be!
   Let Thy goodness, like a fetter,
   Bind my wandering heart to Thee.
   Prone to wander, Lord, I feel it,
   Prone to leave the God I love;
   Here's my heart, O take and seal it,
   Seal it for Thy courts above.

5. O that day when freed from sinning,
   I shall see Thy lovely face;
   Clothèd then in blood washed linen
   How I'll sing Thy sovereign grace;
   Come, my Lord, no longer tarry,
   Take my ransomed soul away;
   Send thine angels now to carry
   Me to realms of endless day.

AMEN.

MUSIC FOUND AT http://www.
freehymnal.com/png/comethoufount.png;
accessed June 3, 2015.

LYRICS TAKEN FROM
Robert Robinson, 1758, *Collection of Hymns
Used by the Church of Christ in Angel Alley,
Bishopgate*, 1759.

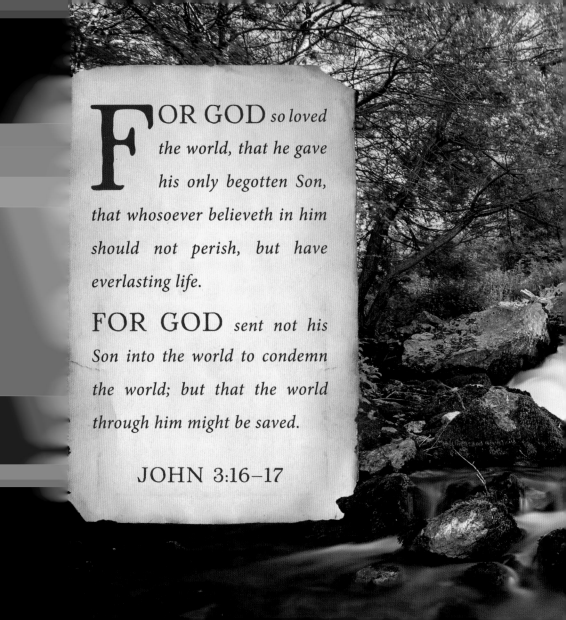

**F**OR GOD *so loved the world, that he gave his only begotten Son, that whosoever believeth in him should not perish, but have everlasting life.*

FOR GOD *sent not his Son into the world to condemn the world; but that the world through him might be saved.*

JOHN 3:16–17

AMEN.

**ANGELA D. BAXTER** is an award-winning graphic designer and the author of *Amazing Grace: Messages of Hope in Scripture and Verse*. She has a love for all hymns, and "Come, Thou Fount of Every Blessing" is one of her favorites. She lives in Utah with her husband, Robert.